The Centenary (
Olton Mere Clu⸤

A History 1899 – 1999

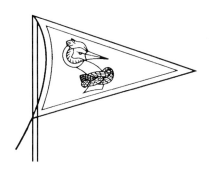

First Published by
Brewin Books Ltd
in February 2000

ISBN 1 85858 162 1

British Library Cataloguing in Publication Data
A Catalogue record for this book is availabe from
the Britsih Library

Typeset in Baskervillle and
made and printed in Great Britain by
SupaPrint (Redditch) Ltd

The Centenary of Olton Mere Club

A History 1899 – 1999

Compiled by
Tel Kilby

BREWIN
BOOKS

FOREWORD

It is impossible to mention by name all the members and friends of Oltom Mere Club who have contributed to this book. However, I must thank Ted Kilby who is responsible for it's production. He has spent a vast amount of time over the past year doing the necessary research and collating the relevant material.
Thanks are also due to Maurice Wells for extracting photographs and other memorabilia from the membership. This book marks the end of the first hundred years of Olton Mere Club. Every effort is being made to ensure it's contining and successful future.

Ted Hill
Chairman

OLTON POOLS

(To G.C.G.)

Now June walks on the waters,
And the cuckoo's last enchantment
Passes from Olton Pools.

Now dawn comes to my window
Breathing midsummer roses,
And scythes are wet with dew.

Is it not strange for ever
That, bowered in this wonder,
Man keeps a jealous heart ? . . .

That June and the June waters,
And birds and dawn-lit roses,
Are gospels in the wind,

Fading upon the deserts,
Poor pilgrim revelations ? . . .
Hist . . . over over Olton pools !

John Drinkwater (1882-1937)

INTRODUCTION

The emergence of Olton Mere Club, as with many other clubs and organisations in the area, was the result of a long and continuous change in the working lives and living conditions of the population, brought about by the Industrial Revolution.

During the 18th century the basic industries of wool and cotton weaving, pot making, leatherwork, mining and metal goods manufacture, were expanding rapidly due, in no small measure, to the emergence of the canals, which transformed the movement of raw materials and finished goods across country.

However, it was the 19th century which was to see the greatest migration of the population in the whole of English History. At the start of the century, eight out of ten people lived or worked in the rural areas. By the end of the century, the population had nearly trebled, when eight out of ten now lived or worked in the towns or urban areas.

They were looking to escape the rigours of farming life, which had been plagued by poor harvests, poor pay and living conditions. The emerging towns and the related job opportunities proved irresistible. The entrepreneurs who helped to create many of the growing factories, were themselves looking to improve the life-style of their families, by moving out to the fringes of the towns. The key to any such move was to be the availability of Public Transport.

Olton Mere was constructed and opened in 1799 by The Warwick and Birmingham Canal Navigation Company as a feeder to replenish the local canal. Built on marshland over a bedrock of Keuper Marl and clay, and fed by Folly Brook, it was designed to have a capacity of one hundred and fifty locks full of water. However, this figure was not achieved at first, and an enlargement was undertaken in 1834; even then the capacity was only one hundred and forty six locks full, or ninety million gallons of water. In the late 1800s a lock keeper's cottage was built and occupied by John Meades until 1899 when the club took on it's first lease on the water.

As with the canals, the creation of the railways nationally and locally, was to have yet another great influence upon events; and when in 1852 the Birmingham to Warwick railway line was opened, followed by the opening of Olton Station in 1864 the scene was set for local expansion.

In anticipation of any movement of the population, many land speculators had purchased large areas of rural land, to be sold off later for housing development.

Most of the land to the north of the Warwick Road was owned by the Josiah Mason Trust, to be developed later by James Kent, a retired Boot and Shoemaker from Snow Hill, who turned builder to develop Warwick Road and Richmond Road.

To the south in an area bounded by Kineton Green Road, Warwick Road and the Mere, William Williams an Ironmaster of Handsworth, purchased the land from five previous owners, to be sold off later at auction during 1869 and 1872.

From these sales Windmill Road was created in 1869 later to be re-named in 1872 as St. Bernards Road.

By 1899 a large number of houses had been completed including St. Margarets' Church (1880). With their families settled in, the householders, particularly those in St. Bernards Road had the money and time to indulge in the pastime of their choosing. Many of whom knew each other as business acquaintances, members of the same Dining Club or as fellow commuters on the train.

Most of the residents were professional men. Of these three were Accountants, four were Jewellers, five Doctors, seven Merchants, one Draper, one Gunsmith and one Engineer.

Prominent amongst those who helped to found local organisations were: Rev. Arthur Butler – Vicar of St. Margarets', James Kent, Harry Harthill, George Godfrey and James Heaton.

Local organisations to emerge before the end of the century were: Penny Savings Bank 1879, Olton Cricket Club and Olton R.U. Football Club, Olton Choral Society 1890, Olton Chess Club, The Mothers Union and Olton Golf Club 1893, Olton Hockey Club, and Olton Mere Club 1899.

INDEX

Olton Mere Club

On the initiative of five residents of St. Bernard's Road, OLTON
MERE CLUB was conceived. They were, John Florence (Claremont
No. 29 St. Bernard's Road), James Heaton (Deerhurst No. 26),
George Godfrey (Tansor House No. 58), Harry Harthill (The Briars
No. 69) and E. Grice (Sunnyside No. 52), who signed a fourteen year
lease on the sporting rights of the mere, dated 25th December 1899.
This date is interesting insofar that although it was the custom to date
legal documents on religious festival and quarter days, this day, until
1752, was also New Year's Day.
Once the lease was signed, it was decided to invite a further five
residents to become Subscribing Members. Those nominated by the
Lessees were Col. Barker (St. Thomas No. 36), J. Griffin (Ericsholme
No. 30), J. Grice (Sunnyside No. 52), E. Fordred (Sedgemere No. 39)
and H. Higgins (Fairfield, Old Warwick Road). Each paid £15 to
share in the privileges of membership, which included, boating,
bathing, fishing and shooting; but were not entitled to any proceeds
from skating or any other income.
The lease also included the occupation of what had previously been
the Mere Keeper's Cottage. Mark Mintram a local gardener by trade,
was appointed part-time Club Warden. He and his wife Anne moved
in early in 1900. They were paid five shillings per week, (25 pence).
John Heaton was elected the first Secretary, and George Godfrey,
Chairman and Treasurer. Membership extended to wives and family
who had to be accompanied at all times, they were, however,
excluded from shooting activities.
Initially rules were few and simple:
> Members were permitted to bathe at any time.
> Visitors (when allowed) were to bathe only from recognised
> places, and then not later than 8.30 am.
> No more than fifteen gentlemen to bathe at any one time.
> The use of soap was not allowed.
> Members to pay Mrs. Mintram 1d. per head for tea in the

Cottage, (minimum 4d. per sitting).
Subscriptions due 1st. June each year.
Resignations to be notified in writing on or before 1st
October.

Here then was set the guidelines of the Mere Club, little did the
Lessees know how the Club would develop. That having survived
two World Wars, periods of drought, low water levels, excessive weed
growth, vandalism and some public outcry for public access, that the
Club would be in the healthy state it is today; but then hindsight is a
wonderful asset.

What follows is more of a record than a story as most of the
participants have either left the Club, or are no longer with us.
Contributions have however been received from a few members with
very diverse memories of the Club. Such as John Riley a Life
Member recalling his entry to the membership in 1936, relates that
you were invited in those days, you did not apply, and the 'benign
oligarchy' or committee, let you in.

John was a keen sailor, and also an avid bird watcher, and
contributed the list of water birds seen over the years. The late John
Baugh, another former Life Member, shortly before his death kindly
contributed the piece about the toilets, both in the Club house and in
his back garden, on the edge of the Mere. Frank Dixon a former
Lessee and Treasurer of the Club, remembers particularly the major
extension to the Club house, the construction of the large launching
ramp, and the removal of excessive weed growth from the water by
boats. Geoff Ward has also provided valuable information on the
construction of the extended Club house. Bob Beach and Mike
Savidge kindly related the history of Solihull School sailing on the
Mere, Ted Hill for memorabilia of the Sailing Club, Dave Florence
for his contribution on the Junior Sailors, Margaret Barber for the
history of the Sea Rangers, Tom Jennings for finding a clue to a Lost
Warden, in the Malverns, Don Blakeley for finding the 'lost Minute
Books' and the notes on the Investment Club, and finally to Maurice
Wells for encouraging members to contribute, and acting as 'leg-
man', by obtaining information from everywhere. The information
contributed by these individuals is much appreciated, and together
with records from the old Club Minute Books and collected archive

information, a record has been compiled to make not only a true history of Olton Mere Club, but hopefully make it also interesting to the reader.

Mark & Anne Mintram

Estate

When the Club took it's first lease on the Mere in 1899, it was exactly one hundred years to the month after it was constructed. The head bank was still of soft construction, and the railway crossed over the head of the Mere, supported by a four hundred foot long bridge of wooden construction. With the widening of both the railway and the Warwick Road between 1930 and 1934, the Mere length was consequently shortened, and concrete walling and culverts were installed. The wooden bridge to be replaced by the steel structure we see today.

First railway bridge across the Mere. c.1907

The cottage built about 1880 had been occupied by the Mere keeper on behalf of the Canal Co. The present boathouse was there at the takeover, but interestingly is not one of the two that were recorded in 1834.

Maintenance of the banks, boundary fences and the trees would remain the first line responsibility of the Canal Co. in maintaining an adequate volume of water, in order to replenish any losses in the local canal. Security on site, and the protection of the wildlife would be the responsibility of the Club. Additionally the Club undertook the responsibility of protecting the interests of the local residents whose properties bordered on the Mere.

The first action of the Lessees was to erect a footbridge over the inlet stream, to be followed by the placement of three bench seats around the Mere for the benefit of the walkers. Small amounts of tree pollarding would be carried out by the Club, but in 1904 a request to create a Trout Rearing Pool was approved and required the felling of twenty trees on the railway bankside.

The bankside in winter

During these early years a bathing pier had been put in place, and a summer arbor was purchased for use as a changing room for the female bathers, and was located in amongst the trees opposite Florence Bay. Skating which had been popular on the Mere for many years previously, was encouraged by the Club, who purchased a ticket kiosk, and placed it near the Mere entrance and charged for admission.

Florence Bay showing second Boathouse, now demolished

The Mere estate originally included all the land in front of the cottage to the Warwick Road. This field was originally rented out to a local beekeeper. Additionally a second field, located at what is now the entrance of the West Warwickshire Club, was also rented to Olton Cricket Club to graze their horse.

Estate matters were low key until the 1930s, when in 1931 the Great Western Railway purchased a strip of land, extending the whole length of the Mere, to increase the number of railtracks from two to four, and this was followed in 1933 with the loss of some of the forecourt, to enable the widening of the Warwick Road.

Some Club members had their own private entrance to the Mere (by agreement), however, trespassers were reported from time to time, and as a result in 1933 the local Constable having been notified, was

6

instructed by his superiors not to patrol the grounds alone. This situation was to last for two years before the problem was solved.

1935 was the year of the first reported incident of pollution, and it was not to be the last. The Committee decided in 1939 to appoint a Grounds Committee under the Chairmanship of G.H. Heaton, their first action was to engage a part-time handyman at a wage of ten shillings (fifty pence) per week. In this same year a fishing stand was erected, and R. Padmore kindly presented a pair of wrought iron gates to the Club, to be erected at the top of the steps at the Mere entrance.

Activities during the second World War were few, due partly to the absence of members on military service, or to far more pressing needs on the Home Front. In 1940 on the directions of the Local Defence Authority, a floating boom was placed across the Mere to prevent enemy aircraft from landing. During the same year the Royal Air Force located a Barrage Balloon and crew at the rear of No. 44 St. Bernard's Road, on the edge of the Mere. Two bombs were dropped within the Mere grounds during the period 1939-45, which was the only damage sustained by enemy action in six years.

The years following the war proved to be very difficult for managing the estate, or to make forward plans, due firstly that the lease was down to one year only, secondly that the Local Council was under great pressure to release land local to the Mere for building development. Additionally a small but strong group of local protesters were campaigning to open the Mere to public access. Each of these potential difficulties were resolved to the benefit of the Club. The number of access members was increasing by 1951, and in consequence two further benches were placed around the Mere.

During the 1950s the Angling Section was increasing in numbers, in consequence a Rod Room was bought and located in the car park in 1956. The 1960s were to be remembered for water pollution problems, which occurred in 1960, 1963, 1964 and in 1966 when the Mere had to be closed temporarily, to prevent the fish disease spreading. Meanwhile the Council were widening Grange Road and a further strip of land was lost. The Sailing Section Workshop was installed in 1963 to replace what had previously been a second hand garage. Similarly the Rod Room was replaced in 1966 with a large hut.

Demonstrations occurred again in 1968 and 1970 to "Save the Mere" (for access to the public) which in 1974 were joined by the local branch of the Young Liberals who threatened to blockade the entrance to the Mere, however, on the day, the support was poor and the protest failed.

1973 and 1974 were excellent years for fishing, and it was also in 1973 that further land was lost for the construction of the Bromford Flats, fronting the Warwick Road. Before this date the Club had obtained a long extension of the lease, which resulted in the Club commissioning the major extension of the clubhouse, which was completed in 1975, to be followed in 1978 with the resurfacing of the car park. All through the 1970s the Angling Section had been constructing permanent fishing platforms on the bankside, and by 1980 forty had been completed.

One of the many well constructed fishing platforms

Launching boats on to the water can at times be difficult, especially when the levels of the park and the water are both much lower than the bankside. Several ramps have been constructed over the years, however, in 1980 a major ramp construction was undertaken, giving great benefit to all members with boats to be launched from the main boat park. Floodlighting was installed in the car park in 1992, improving access and security at night. During the remainder of the eighties, with Club membership growing, greater use of the clubhouse was made for social events, which included dancing on the green, and Bar-b-Qs. Water pollution and excessive weed growth were continuing problems to be dealt with, although sailing was not severely disrupted, in fact this was the decade when junior and lady members were beginning to make their presence felt at all levels. Regular monthly fishing contests were now being held, some further fish re-stocking took place, and 1983 and 1984 provided some of the best fishing for years.

The nineties mirrored previous decades insofar that there has been a mixture of water pollution from green alga in 1996, with some vandalism in the same year, with the loss of some boat equipment, and a six week total interruption of all sport late in 1998, due to the work of increasing the bank height all round the Mere, to prevent flooding in the surrounding area.

The Fishing Section updated their accommodation still further with the purchase of a cabin, which members converted into a Fishing Lodge, which was formally opened in 1995 by Life Member - George Hill.

The Club, now with over three hundred members, and having leased and maintained this stretch of water for one hundred years, can be proud of it's condition; not only the water but also the trees and the bankside vegetation. The original Lessees would no doubt be both surprised and proud of the Club they created, without knowing of all the work put in over the years by all those members, who turned up to help with bank clearance, construction of fishing platforms, ramps, pontoons, the O.D. Hut and Boathouse, and even decoration of the clubhouse.

Clubhouse

From 1899 when the Cottage was taken over as part of the lease of the mere, not only was this to be the home for the Warden and his family, but the meeting place of the Lessees who used the lounge for their deliberations. The Clubhouse as it exists today, did not evolve until 1958, when the first building programme took place as an add-on to the Cottage.

Cottage and Clubhouse from dinghy park

Subscribing members could also take tea here on Sundays, with the added luxury of a coal fire in the winter months from 1900. Annie Mintram provided tea at 1d. (less than 1/2p) per cup, with a minimum of 4d. per sitting.

Other facilities in the cottage were very basic, whether for living or just taking tea. Lighting was by oil lamp, cold water was drawn from the hand pump in the garden, and the toilet was an outside privvy, also in the garden c/w wooden bench seat and a large galvanised bucket. The late John Baugh used to repeat the tale 'that once the bucket was full the contents were deposited close to the railway bridge, and there grew possibly the largest rhododendrons for miles around'. As will be revealed later, for a selected few much better facilities would be available courtesy of John Heaton.

After twelve months occupation a new firegrate and hearth was installed at a cost of five pounds five shillings and four pence.

Little or no change occurred after this initial activity until 1939, however, Mark Mintram was still there in the cottage, looking after members interests and Annie was still serving tea. This was also the year when a full members meeting was held in the cottage for the first time, for which a drinks licence was obtained.

As the number of boats was increasing at this time, a problem of storing masts was solved by removing the ceiling over the passageway in the cottage.

However, by 1947 and after the Second World War, there was still no piped water, electricity or a flushing toilet. The subject of toilets was to appear in the Sailing Club Minutes for nearly ten years. There was a salvation, however, for those members who were taken short, but 'knew the ropes'. The late John Baugh recalled 'When he was thinking of buying 26 St. Bernard's Road, the then owner John Heaton, told him that membership of the Mere Club went with the house – as it were, including the Secretaryship'. He thought that this last bit seemed ominous, but as he was not too forthcoming he settled the purchase, but was soon to find out that his outside lavatory had always been considered to be for use by the Club members, who had no facilities of their own.

Anyone wanting the Secretary would stroll up the garden, past the revolving Summer House where Heaton's poor tubercular daughter used to live (following the sun around), and into the house. This was tolerated for some years until a flushing toilet was installed in the cottage in 1956. Presumably to the great relief of all concerned.

The end of the nineteen fifties saw at last the installation of electricity and a flushing toilet; drinks purchase by chit was also introduced at this time, but the major event of the decade was the creation of the 'Clubhouse' as an extension to the cottage, at a cost of £184 and was opened by the Club Chairman, C.J. Hurst on the 27th July 1958. With the increasing use of the new clubhouse in the 1960s including many more visitors to the Club, a payphone was installed, and the Warden put cigarettes on sale. It became evident after five more years in 1963 that even more space was required to accommodate members in the clubhouse. Consequential enlargement would include a full width bay window feature complete with replacement roof and flooring, designed by Michael Harper. At a cost of £1108 the extension was completed in 1964.

During the following five years bench seats were installed in the bay window, an additional toilet fitted and a gas cooker purchased. Phil Rodway donated the first Sailing Competition Records Boards.

Membership was approaching one hundred and twenty by 1970, and again more visitors were being entertained, particularly from local Sailing Clubs and Schools. Having obtained a thirty year extension to the lease, the General Committee decided to put in hand a further major extension to the clubhouse. A Building Sub-Committee was formed under the chairmanship of L.J. Farrow; and Phillip Skelcher was asked to prepare a design. The plan was to include a bar, lounge, games room, male and female changing rooms with showers, and additional toilets, all on two levels.

Costs were estimated at over nine thousand pounds, this would be met by a combination of a bank loan and a second interest-free loan from a small number of Club members.

Work started in 1974 and was completed in August 1975 at a cost of £9259 including Calor Gas heating. The Grebe Club donated carpets, tables and armchairs, and the internal decoration was completed by a team of members led by Len Robinson.

Before the end of the decade, Real Ale was introduced, as was a Pool table. The final act was the installation of small-bore central heating. In spite of this major change and further cosmetic improvements, bar takings began to fall in the early eighties, even as low a fifteen pounds on some days. In consequence Saturday opening was introduced. This change together with other actions taken by the Bar Committee including refurbishment of the lounge, retrieved the situation.

Today as we enter the New Century, the clubhouse is being used more than ever. The third enlargement in 1975 was certainly the right decision taken by the General Committee, which has not only enabled the Social Committee to hold many of their events 'on site', but also allowed the Club to offer visitors the sort of hospitality they would expect from one of the better Sports Clubs.

The Sunken Narrowboat

Skating

Skating on the Mere probably goes back to the beginning of the nineteenth century when the Mere was created.

However, it was not until the 1880s when the local population began to increase through the construction of many houses in St. Bernards and Kineton Green Roads and elsewhere that skating really took off. Originally skating events were organised to support both St. Margaret's Church Building Fund and charities to support the poor. Once the Mere Club was formed, regular annual sessions were organised, in fact a small Ticket Kiosk was purchased, to continue to allow the general public to use this facility, dependant upon the weather. Records show that from 1900 the winters were consistently cold, such that each February or March a spell of skating could be organised. It was considered that a thickness of ice of no less than eight or nine inches (twenty/twenty three centimetres) was safe.

First year attendances were excellent and spaced over a five day period in February. Gross income was £50.11s.10d. and based upon an estimated entrance fee of sixpence, and allowing for skate hire charges, it would seem that between one thousand and fifteen hundred skaters enjoyed this event.

These sessions continued well into the 1930s with attendances and income varying with the duration of the cold spells; but usually it was over two to five days. Skating sessions during the evening darkness were held on a number of occasions, when warning lights were placed around the Mere to mark danger areas and submerged trees etc. Skaters were encouraged to carry candle-lit Chinese Style Lanterns and to form long chains of skaters to add to the enjoyment. It is of interest to note that in 1917 (Feb. 5th) the lowest temperature recorded locally was TWO DEGREES FAHRENHEIT (thirty degrees of frost) followed in 1929 with a recorded low of ONE DEGREE FAHRENHEIT.

By 1939 the Ticket Kiosk was still in use, and by this date charges were being made for parking, namely one shilling for cars and sixpence for motor-cycles.

The tradition of donating part of the income to charity continued, and it is interesting to note that in 1941 the benefiting charity was the Russian Red Cross.

Entrance fees were discontinued in 1945 when the Club realised the Public Liability Risk, should an accident occur, after visitors had paid to enter. In spite of this change the British Red Cross still received a cheque for £30.

Skating, similar to bathing has been an under reported pastime, particularly on the Mere as most of the activity was by individual skaters, rather than groups in competition. Not since the 1950s have the Club organised open skating sessions.

Today this is a facility no longer offered, as it was in the early years of the Club, to the general public; particularly as the period of 'Safe Ice Days' continue to decrease, and that the Public Liability Risk is too great to be considered.

Public skating session c1907

Bathing

Bathing in the Mere was possibly the most popular pastime enjoyed by Club members and visitors in the early years. In spite of severe winters it would seem that there were sufficient days when the water temperature was high enough for bathing in comfort.

During the first year a Bathing Pier was purchased and put in place, and the Bathing Rules laid down. Members and their families, who were to be accompanied, were allowed to bathe at any time. Local residents, having obtained permission could bathe but no later than 8.30a.m. and then only from recognised bathing points.

Access to the Mere was to be through the proper entrances only, (some members already having created private gateways at the bottom of their gardens). Up to fifteen gentlemen would be allowed to bathe at one time, soap could not be used.

A Summer Arbor was purchased in 1902 and placed in amongst the trees on the railway bankside for use as a changing point for the female bathers. Many years later a well known male member would comment, "that it was large enough for changing, but too small for making love". Finally this Arbor was burnt down, when supposedly a spark from a passing Steam Train set fire to the thatched roof. But then there are those who suggest that it caught fire by the heat generated from the inside, on an occasion when there was a mixed bathing session.

By 1938 two Bathing Huts existed, and later in 1948, G.H. Heaton offered his Launch 'Dipper' to the Club, C.J. Hurst paid the £25 asking price and presented it to the Club for use by the Junior Bathers.

Many local people have probably swam in the Mere over the years, and typically one resident of St. Bernards Road is reported in 1950 to have swam the width of the Mere daily before breakfast. A bathing raft was put in place during 1951, and a second in 1955. This was the last recorded act of the Committee, on behalf of the bathers. In 1959 however, the West Midlands and Handsworth Swimming Clubs were allowed to hold a One Mile Swim in the Mere.

Finally in 1969 after a period of seventy years of bathing and swimming, complaints were received that nude swimmers had been seen in the Mere. It had to be assumed that in fact they were intruders, as no Club member was honest or brave enough to accept responsibility.

Today bathing in the Mere is non-existent, due to the fact that bankside facilities no longer exist, and that both Public and Private Swimming Pools are now available locally, with water temperatures at a much more agreeable level than those experiences in the Mere at almost any time of the year.

A Typical Snowscene

Shooting

Whilst shooting was one of four sporting pastimes offered to members from the inception of the Club, it was possibly the least popular.

The area bounded by the Warwick Road, Kineton Green Road and Grange Road was before and after the Mere was constructed a haven for wild rabbits. In fact Grange Road (previously named Folly Lane) was known locally as Bunny Lane.

With the construction of the Mere and the planting of the bankside trees by 1899, the opportunity for shooting both rabbits and wildfowl, would have been an attraction to prospective members.

The Club Records do not show any activity that required the attention of the Lessees until 1925, when one year's ban on shooting was imposed, due to the reported absence of wildfowl. Whether this absence was due to natural causes or due to excessive shooting is not known. However, the following year, a one day's ferreting session was sanctioned, following complaints by local residents that the rabbits were eating their garden plants.

The shooting ban was to continue until 1929. What transpired after the ban was lifted is not known. Whether the gunmen or the rabbits prevailed over the following twenty years is only indicated by an application to shoot rabbits in 1949 was refused.

A deviation from the original concept of shooting at the Mere occurred in 1941 when a R.A.F. Barrage Balloon Crew, stationed on the edge of the Mere, were reported for the indiscriminate use of air rifles. The situation was promptly corrected by the Club Chairman Phil Rodway.

Shooting has not been an 'option' of membership now for more than fifty years, and has never been an option for lady members, or wives and daughters of members.

By the time the Second World War was over, and the Mere Fishing and Sailing Sections had been formed, the Mere grounds had been almost totally enclosed by private houses. Therefore the wildlife habitat, the types of sporting pastime, and the size of the membership had dramatically changed – all to the exclusion of shooting.

Each to His Own

Fishing

Fishing was one of the premier reasons for the original lessees creating the OLTON MERE CLUB. The committee asked John Florence to formulate a set of fishing rules for members to follow. Rod and line was the only method to be used, and then only one rod at one time. All fish caught under specified weights/sizes were to be returned to the water immediately, such as pike under 4lb., bream, carp and tench 2lb., roach 7 inches, perch 3/4lb or 9 inches.

These rules would suggest that larger fish could be taken and contest fishing was not envisaged at the time.

Early in 1900 one thousand five hundred perch were placed in the Mere at a cost of £9.0s.0d. plus £2.0s.0d. carriage, to be followed by one hundred and fifty rudd and one hundred bream in 1901, courtesy of John Florence. In the same year the local canal was netted and again the fish were placed in the Mere, at a cost of £1.10s.0d.

The quality of fishing that followed the introduction of these fish is unknown, however, in 1904 it was decided to try to develop trout fishing in the Mere. A number of trees were felled on the railway bankside by the Canal Co. at a cost of £4.5s.3d. to enable a trout rearing pool to be created.

Meanwhile pike fishing was encouraged and any caught were to be removed. Preparations began, and later one thousand mature rainbow trout were placed in the Mere, courtesy of Messrs. Florence and Fordred. After six months fishing, not one trout had been caught; in consequence the whole project was abandoned.

In spite of this setback, fishing continued, and course fish stocks multiplied. In 1916 a specimen golden bream weight 6lbs. was caught by J.V. Worthington, and is now displayed in the clubhouse. Was this fish one of the thousand introduced in 1901? Similarly of the pike that seemed to thrive on the trout in the early years, was the specimen weighing twenty three and a half pounds and caught by Charles Hodson in 1926 also one of them? This fish is also to be seen in the clubhouse.

They don't all get away

The Mere was netted in 1929 by the Birmingham Piscatorial Society when some thirty thousand small fish were removed, and eight hundred mature roach were introduced at a cost of £5.7s.6d.

Pollution of the water has, over the years, been a problem. In 1935 and 1944 land drainage from local site developments were the problem; in 1963 and 1972 Canadian Pond Weed was the culprit. Frank Dixon a life member and former Treasurer of the Club recalls that the problem was so severe that working parties were towed out in punts by the rescue launch, the weed was lifted by hand had to be deposited in piles on the bankside. This operation had to be repeated several times during the season, before the problem could be overcome.

In 1966 Columnar's Disease caused the Mere to be closed temporarily to prevent it spreading further. By coincidence this was the same year that a quantity of fish were transferred into the Mere from a pool at Shard End. By contrast 1973 and 1975 were recorded as the best for fishing for many years.

For the first forty years fishing was mainly by individuals trying their luck from the bankside or from the Club punts. In 1939 the General Committee decided to appoint an Angling and Grounds Committee, to oversee subscriptions, fishing and the control of vermin. Subscriptions were increased and nine new members were recruited as a consequence. A fishing stand was also provided at this time.

As with sailing, fishing at the Mere did not expand until after the Second World War. 1945 was the year that the Fishing Section was formed. C. Bloomer was the first elected Chairman, and J. Wilday the Secretary. The ordering of a third Club fishing punt was one of the first actions, bringing the total of Club boats to four, which included a rowing dinghy. Members would be allowed to bring nine visitors a year, but only two at any one time.

On July 19th 1947 the Club held it's first Inter-Club Contest against Olton British Legion. Membership had by now increased to twenty five, and with a grant of twenty five pounds from the General Committee, the Club stocked the water with two hundred roach.

Through the fifties membership was expanding, and two more rowing dinghies were purchased. However, in 1952 the Club Rules had to be amended, due to some members who being in arrears with their subscriptions, were fishing as guests of other paid-up members. By 1956 the membership reached forty five, and a rod room was purchased and erected in the car park. Part of the expansion was by junior members, in response the committee formulated the first Club Rules for Juniors aged 14 to 21 years, followed by the organisation of the first Junior Fishing Contest.

For the second time in the history of the Mere, the introduction of trout was being considered, and in 1960 the Club Rules were amended to cover the differing trout season, this was followed by the placement of 1,000 trout into the water. Initially the project went well and a fair number of fish were caught in the first year. However, in the second and third years catches dropped dramatically, and further planned stocking was deferred.

With three years of excessive weed growth, one year of severe fish disease, and two years of low water levels the 1960s saw the Fishing Section taking positive action to combat the problems. For three years the water was chemically treated to control the weed growth, to be followed by a re-stocking programme. Firstly 400 bream were introduced in 1968, followed by 230 carp and 700 tench in 1969, and a further re-introduction of 1,000 trout in 1971. Again the fishing started well, and in spite of another spate of excessive weed growth in 1971, a further 500 trout were added in 1972. What followed was four excellent fishing years, mixed with two very hot summers, two more years of excessive weed growth, and four years of water pollution or fish disease. The third attempt to introduce trout failed. It was not to be until 1984 that a longer trouble-free period of fishing was to be experienced.

This is no time to panic

At the start of these difficult times, membership dropped to fourteen, followed by some committee resignations in 1968. However, the situation was recovered initially by some publicity, the replacement of the rod room with a fishing hut, and the progressive construction of some forty permanent fishing stands around the Mere, which resulted in the membership rising to seventy in 1981, and further

entry was closed.
With the return to better fishing in the 80s, the Club embarked upon a plan to protect the fish stock. In 1984 it was decided to ban keep-nets, except in bona-fide contests, and only barbless hooks would be allowed in the popular sizes. A further 100 carp were introduced in 1985, and membership had now risen to eighty. Although 1986 was a year of low water, a programme of lily planting was carried out, in and around Florence Bay, to the direct benefit of the carp and tench. 1987 saw the introduction of 100 tench and 200 rudd, to be followed finally in 1988 with 50 carp.

The water retreats – the fishermen follow

Pike have been in the Mere since the Mere Club began, and probably long before. An effort to remove them in 1904 with rod and line failed, and since then they have flourished on the 'stock' of smaller course fish that have bred naturally in the Mere, or on the trout that were 'tried out' on three occasions. Twice over the years pike have been blamed for the lack of fish caught, only to be exonerated when netting showed the fish to be there but reluctant to bite. Piking contests continue to be held, and the size and condition of the fish caught is usually a good indicator of the health of the whole fish stock. Records show that in the 1987/88 season, thirty nine pike were caught and returned, of which sixteen were over ten pounds in weight, and in 1988/89, sixty four fish were recorded, and this time thirty eight were over ten pounds. All in very good condition and testimony to the efforts of the Fishing Section in trying to keep a balance of quality and quantity, to meet the aspirations of it's members.

1989 was the year that the office of Club President was reinstated, and Dr. P.J. Barber was duly elected, having served as Chairman for twenty one years.

Raising money for charity has long been a tradition at the Club, and the former St. Christophers Home for Children, The Red Cross the N.S.P.C.C. amongst others have benefitted in the past, and some continue to benefit from money raised at charity contests.

Not surprisingly, fishing tackle, methods and baits used have changed over the past one hundred years. Rods have moved from hollow to split cane, to steel and the fibreglass, up to today's materials of carbon fibre and boron, reducing weights down to a few ounces. With lines now made from synthetic materials, giving small diameters and increased strength, together with chemically hardened and machine sharpened hooks, the choice of price and quality is wide.

However, changes in baits used over the years have been exceeded only by changes in method. Today the use of the swimfeeder, and the long pole, with lengths exceeding sixteen metres, have influenced both individual and contest fishermen more than any other development.

The original Lessees set the minimum for the weight and size for what they considered specimen fish being caught in the Mere at that time. Namely, pike 4lbs., bream, carp and tench 2lbs., roach and perch 12 ounces. By comparison the heaviest fish caught and recorded to date are, pike 20lbs. 4oz., bream 5lbs., carp 20 lbs., tench 3lbs. 14oz. and perch 2lbs. 13oz.

It is therefore testimony to all those members who have contributed to the care and maintenance of the waters, that the present list, held by the Club, of specimen fish caught over recent years that all species (except trout) are thriving, and the larger fish being caught are gaining in average weight.

Sailing

Sailing Through the Century

The level of sailing activity as experienced in 1999 on the Mere goes back to 1946, when keen sailing members decided to form their own Sub-Committee. As with the Fishing Club a determined few were to create a specific section for their sport. Events over the following fifty odd years, in growth and achievement have proved what a landmark decision this was in the history of both the Sailing Section and the Mere Club itself.

However, sailing on the Mere goes much further back than 1946. Whilst boats have been on the Mere since it's construction in 1799, their use for pleasure would seem to date from the 1830s as evidenced by the Survey Map of J. Whorrall which shows two boathouses. A single boathouse may indicate a maintenance craft was kept 'on site', as enlargement was still being carried out of the Mere as late as 1834. However, two boathouses would indicate that some form of pleasure boating or sailing was enjoyed from this time onwards.

First Club Boathouse c.1912

Regular sailing started on the Mere as a sport for individuals who were, at the turn of the century, privileged to have the time and money to indulge in a sport or pastime, particularly if it happened to be right on their 'doorstep'. With total membership never exceeding fifty for nearly half a century, competitive races were almost non existent. Launching was easy, and boat parking presented no difficulty, especially to those members whose gardens touched the edge of the Mere. Little or nor written records exist of sailing activities on the Mere until the 1940s. An item from the Minute Books dated 1904 relates to "buoys being purchased to mark the shallows and submerged trees to ensure safe sailing".

As with the Fishing Club, sailing only 'came alive' after the Second World War. During 1945 the General Committee were considering Sailing Races, and copies of the Royal Yacht Association Rules were circulated to all members. Dr. D.R. Cartwright offered to provide a Silver Challenge Cup for such competition. Following this initiative sailing members formed their own Sailing Section on 29th April 1946, the inaugural meeting being attended by Messrs. Drew, Heaton, Padmore and Rodway. Navigation lights were presented later by Mr. A. Gaydon, which would indicate sailing on occasions continued until after dark.

Several new boats were ordered from Faireys in 1947, all to be built to the same specification. During this year and in 1948 the average number of boats starting in races was five, despite the fact that by now five trophies were up for competition, given by Dr. Cartwright, J.R. Padmore, G. Heaton and McCartney-Filgate. Handicap races were soon established with the Wildcat being the most popular craft.

At the end of 1949 the first Annual Dinner was held at the Fleur de Lys, Lowsonford. Tickets were fifteen shillings (seventy five pence) including drinks at the Clubhouse beforehand. This event was followed in subsequent years by visits to the Red Lion, Knowle and the Kings Head, Aston Cantlow.

Easier launching of boats on to the water was helped by the construction of a slipway in 1951, followed by the purchase of a launching trolley in 1952. A powered launch 'Little Mist' was made available to the Club as a rescue boat in 1955 by Commodore Phil Rodway. 1957 was the year of the first Open Day, which included sailing, rowing, swimming and in the evening dancing on the green with a barbecue.

Three Wild Cats

The ramp from the boat park – completed 1980

The age limit for Junior Membership was lowered in 1958 from 16 to
14 years, also a sailing dinghy was purchased for instructional

purposes. During 1959 Solihull School began to use the Mere regularly every week, and the construction of a ramp from the car park eased launchings for everybody. Forty boats was the Club water limit at this time, and the first successful Winter Trials were carried out in this same year.

Following the success of the Open Day in 1957, it is decided to hold a Water Sports Day in 1961. Events not only included sailing and boating but canoeing and a water ski-ing demonstration.

The O.D. Hut (originally a platform with a chair on it) which has played such an important part in the Club over the years was completed in 1962, at a cost of £75, at the same time a second launching trolley was purchased (for Fireflies). With the number of boats increasing, and more members choosing to carry out their own boat repairs, a workshop was erected in the car park in 1963. Solos were tried out for the first time during this year. Average turnout per race through the season was only five boats, however the Laying-Up Supper was attended by no less than one hundred and ten members and guests.

Sailing the following year was temporarily transferred to Earlswood Lakes due to the low water levels. A new Rescue Launch 'Lilliput' was purchased, and again Phil Rodway showed his generosity by presenting to the Club his Launch 'Roddy'. Now restored and held by Solihull School.

Development work on the Warwick Road at this time had caused many boats to vacate the boat park, and it was through the kindness of John Baugh allowing the use of the orchard at the bottom of his garden that the potential problem was solved. By this time the boats returned, the park had been concreted and the boat limit raised to forty five.

A Dell Quay Dory rescue boat was delivered in 1968 c/w Johnson outboard motor at a cost of £450. Vandalism occurred for the first time and two dinghies were damaged. The boat limit was again raised to forty eight in 1970, and electrical communication between the Clubhouse and the O.D. Hut as installed.

During all this time since the start of the Club, successive committees had been overseeing the 'day to day' running of the Club. Once the programme for each season had been finalised the real work began. Dates and start times had to be confirmed, particularly if outside

Low water – October 1964

clubs were involved, and special transport arrangements laid on where required. Due notice had to be given to all possible contestants, and notices and course details duly posted in the Clubhouse before each event. Meanwhile the Safety Officer will have been checking the safety boats, ensuring that the engines are running well, that fuel and oil stocks were adequate. Meanwhile the Harbour Master would have ensured that the surface of the pontoons are safe underfoot, that all buoyancy floats were functioning and all tie-up ropes are in place, and the O.D. Box fully operational. The Sailing Master will have ensured that the Course Plan had been posted, that the buoys have been positioned and the Officer of the Day is nominated and in attendance. In between race days these officers together with Fleet Captains will have been overseeing the care and maintenance of Club boats, boat parks, ramps and walkways, usually by organising working parties of enthusiastic members. It is this organisation coupled with the enthusiasm of members that has ensured the continuing success of the Club.

The dinghy park was holding 70 boats in 1978, the same year that the Firefly Fleet was replaced by the Handicap Fleet. With so many boats on the park, the Club embarked, in 1980, on the construction of a major size ramp, from the park over the bankside and down into the water, at a cost of £3,300, most of the work being carried out by Club members. The Lark Fleet was also established in this year.

Solihull School celebrated twenty one years sailing on the Mere also in 1980. An event recorded at the time with a presentation of a plaque, to the Mere Club, and which currently hangs over the bar in the Clubhouse. Twenty one boats turned out on Boxing Day that year, for the Brass Monkey Race, followed in 1981 with the best sailing season for many years, including a turnout of forty boats for the Cadet Open Meeting.

Continuous attention was required as to the parking of boats, if only to separate the 'dead' boats from the 'live', and in 1982 the park was extended to allow this operation to take place. Two severe winters followed, with low water in each Spring of 1984 and 1985. Membership was falling in 1986, when the Club was given the opportunity to share a stand at the N.E.C. Boat Show to try and recruit more members who would be offered a 'trial acquaintance session' before taking up full membership.

1988 saw some of the best sailing for six years, sailors as young as six years old were now sailing as part of the Optimist Fleet. Seventeen boats were out on the first day of sailing in 1989, and fourteen Cadets took part in the Open event. A glass-fibre Cadet was purchased as a Club training boat to expand this fleet further. Membership for that year was eventually closed. It was, however, decided to appear again at the N.E.C. due to the good response received following the 1986 show.

Training being an essential part of the Club, a Narwal power boat was successfully tried out as an instruction craft in 1990. With the Optimist boats becoming increasingly popular, an Optimist Camp was attended by a number of boats at Bala Lake in 1992. This was the year that the last Cadet was sold, a class of boat that had been sailed on the Mere for nearly thirty years, having produced many first class sailors. The following year was to be again one of low water levels, partly due to bank maintenance work; in spite of this problem the sailing programme was completed, including the National 12 boats which now numbered nine. During 1994 some members received sea training at Weymouth, and other members represented the Club at West Kirby, Northampton and Rockley Point Open Meetings.

Lady members had been sailing and competing for the Trustees Cup since 1959, however, in 1995 the committee felt that the current number of lady sailors was far too low, such that a recruiting drive was launched, and the first Lady Committee Member was co-opted. Meanwhile the Junior Sailors were increasingly active and the Mere S.C. held it's first Open Sponsored Meeting for Gold and Silver Fleets with a total of twenty six boats competing. By 1996 the first of the clubs' National 12s began to compete in the Sailing World Team racing event. Following the success of the recruiting drive for lady members, the committee now decided to hold a Ladies Weekend twice yearly. Another first that year was the vintage Open Event, once the PY numbers were sorted out.

The nineties ended with yet again a disruption for bank work in 1998, interrupting sailing for six weeks, as the banking had to be raised to meet new flood protection levels, set by the Government. As before the Club planned it's programme round this event.

Junior Sailing

One of the many reasons for the endurance and success of any Club is the process of involving the younger members in all it's activities. The Mere Sailing Club realised this as early as 1949 when Children's Competitions were organised during school holidays, additionally permission was given to Solihull School for the occasional use of the Mere for sail training, to further encourage juniors to take up the sport.

By 1954 rules were agreed for Junior Sailing Members (14-21 years). Two rowing dinghies were purchased and juniors were allowed berthing for their own Cadet craft, and one visitor for crewing was allowed. The result of these decisions would ultimately see some twenty six local School and Organisations using the Mere for training or competition.

Solihull School

The first junior group outside the Club to train on the Mere were as previously stated, Solihull School. Although occasional use began in 1949, it was not until 1959 that regular weekly sessions started. The initiative came from Bob Beach, the School Biology Master who recalls…

"Enterprises were the boats chosen, such that cotton cruising sails were never used, and the boys went straight on to racing rigs. Some boats were borrowed, a twelve foot with Heron rig from the school naval section, and an eleven foor plus from a parent.

The rescue boat was a well shaped pram rowing dinghy, ideal to teach the important stages of self help in the process of rescue.

Team races against other schools, although slow to start, soon built up a reputation for excitement, and splendid teas afterwards, and a number of unbeaten records. Taking part in Open School Competitions is now part of the calendar. In the end a complete fleet of Enterprises were launched.

For a long time School Sailing was run as a one man band, but improvement in school staffing allowed assistance by John Wall, Ken Hall and Mike Williams. The breakthrough came when Mike Savidge joined the school staff, we were able to build a very strong Club; sailing every Monday, Wednesday and Thursday afternoons. Then came Saturday morning sailing and assistance from Mike Dudgeon and Richard Costard, and help from ex-pupils, especially Ted Hill. Today the tradition continues, with Steve Bromley in charge of sailing. Girls joined the school in the sixth form in 1973, and have taken part since then. There has even been a Girl Captain of Sailing. Old Silhilians now sail all over the world, with an outstanding record of competitive successes. Perhaps the reason is that Olton Mere is an excellent training water, and the windshifts are so numerous as the air comes down over the trees, that they become quick to notice them. Without tides, and enclosed, it is relatively safe; people with modest skills can sail their boats to the limit. Capsizes can be common place without being a dramatic experience.

Solihull School Sailing Club has completed it's first forty years, with hopefully many more to come, and is most grateful for it's association over the years with generous host Olton Mere Club."

Another junior organisation that has long associations with the Mere Club is the local Sea Ranger Group.

Solihull Sea Rangers – SRS Vandyke

Sea Rangers were originally a section of the Girl Guide Association, after finishing Guides at the age of 16, girls could join a Land Ranger, Sea Ranger or Air Ranger Crew, according to the type of activities they were interested in. The Solihull Sea Ranger Crew was founded in 1947, but as the oldest Crew Logbook we have starts in 1951, details of the Crews' earliest history are rather sparse. All Sea Ranger Crews are named after ships. Why the Crew chose the name 'Vandyke' after a merchant steamer commandeered as a troopship in World War II and sunk at the Battle of Narvik, is unknown.

by 1951, when records began, it appears that the Crew had a rowing boat of their own and were already boating on the Mere, although the origin of the first connection is again unknown, it was during 1951 that the Skipper, Miss lee, handed over to Mrs. Ursula (Sue) Hay, who had previously been Skipper of a Sea Ranger Crew in Ladywood. Over the next few years, the Crew acquired a further rowing boat and their first canoe; they were also lent a 14 foot aluminium sailing boat, named Guinea-Pig, which had been built by Mr. Reynolds of Reynolds Tube Co. Ltd.

There follows another gap in the records until the mid 1960s, by which time the Crew had extended its' boats to include another rowing dinghy and a clinker-built sailing dingy, and extended its' activities to include camps, hiking, competitive regattas against other Crews, assault courses etc. Many of these activities were organised jointly with 1st. Olton Venture Scout Unit, and the relationship gradually became closer, culminating in the formation in 1970 of a joint Venture Scout - Sea Ranger Unit. By this time, however, moves towards modernisation were afoot in the Girl Guide Association, and moves were made to abolish specialised Ranger Crews, including Sea Rangers. As a result, a number of Sea Ranger Crews throughout the country decided to form an independent Sea Ranger Association to enable them to continue their Boating based programme. Sue Hay and some of the Rangers left the joint unit and once more became a Sea Ranger Crew, resuming under the name SRS Vandyke. It soon became apparent that there was a demand for extending the age range downwards, and in 1974 the Solihull crew set up their Cadet Sea Ranger section for 10 - 14 year olds, after which the girls would go up to the Sea Ranger section.

Sue Hay remained as Skipper until 1977 when she was succeeded by Mrs. Vera Howes, who was in turn succeeded by Mrs. Margaret

Barber in 1979. Since then the Crew has continued its regular boating activities on the Mere; rowing canoeing and sailing. The old wooden rowing dinghies have been replaced by a 9 foot dinghy and a 16 foot gig and plastic canoes have replaced the wooden-framed canvas ones; but the wooden Gull class sailing dinghy built by the Crew under the watchful eye of one of the then Rangers fathers in 1966, it still in use. Throughout the Crews existence the Olton Mere Club has generously allowed us boating facilities, which has been a major factor in the Crews continuing ability to provide many girls with opportunities for "messing about in boats" which would not otherwise be available to them. We offer them our grateful thanks for all their help and support, and congratulations on their 100th anniversary.

O.M.C. Juniors – Optimist Sailors

In 1988 and 1989 Geoff Sinton was Commodore of the Club. He had been very involved in youth sailing when Cadet boats, for the under 17's, were sailed at the Mere. However, towards the end of the decade the Cadet Fleet had diminished and Geoff gave the go-ahead for a new Optimist Fleet to be started for children over the age of six. During 1988 six families bought half a dozen new Optimist boats from Moores Boatyard in Norfolk. Geoff designed and built the Club Optimist storage rack, which is used by the Club today.

Dave Florence was the first Optimist Fleet Captain, and Phil Worthington was the Training Officer. From these beginnings a comprehensive training programme was devised and implemented. Before long young sailors were representing Olton Mere Club at Open Meetings up and down the country with increasing success. Later Phil became Fleet Captain followed by Russell Cherry, Warwick Hall and Howard Cole.

In 1990 Olton Mere staged it's own Open Meeting, which have continued as an annual event ever since.

Olton Mere Club has produced Optimist sailors who have represented Great Britain. In 1996 Alex Cherry was a member of the National Team at the South African World Championships, and Jonathan Worthington was a member of the British team at the European Championships.

The Club now benefits from having accomplished sailors who have come through the Optimist Training Programme and are now integrated into the 'Club sailing'. Many of the original half dozen boats, which were originally bought to found the Fleet, are still sailed at the Club although the owners have changed. Their original owners having moved on to sail Lasers and National Twelves.

Our children not only benefit from learning to sail as a 'life-skill' but also develop personal confidence, communication skills, self reliance, motivation and independence which can help them succeed in life.

Optimist Fleet sailing is still flourishing at the Mere and has the benefit of enthusiastic leadership through Juliet Olivio as Fleet Captain, Alan Williams, an ex-Optimist sailor, now takes part in regular 'Club sailing', and assists Juliet with the current training programme.

The Club Optimist Sailing Programme is now an integral part of the main Club Sailing Programme.

Junior Sailing into the Future

It is now fifty years since Junior Sailing Events were first organised by the Club, which included holiday events for those still at school.

Over the years some twenty-six schools and organisations have used the Mere for sail training and competition. In addition to Solihull School, Van Dyke Sea Rangers and the Club Juniors, there are also the Cadets from T.S. Gamecock (Shirley) Sea Cadets, the Scouts from 1st Solihull (Nelson) and 279 Birmingham (Hall Green) Sea Scouts, still sailing the Mere.

Many of the juniors of the past have become Club Family Members, and in turn have encouraged their children to take up the sport of sailing.

The future of sailing in the Club is now in the hands (or boats) of these children, to carry forward the successes of the past century into the New Millennium.

Racing

Racing was to be an important part of the future of the Club, and in 1947 the office of Honorary Sailing Master was created, and F.B. Parsons was the first appointee. A sailor of long experience, he was also to be responsible for training. Within the first year of this appointment twelve race meetings had been organised, and the average turnout was five boats. Initial races commenced on May

12th and the entrance fee two shillings and six pence (twelve and half new pence). Three minute intervals was the rule, and a silver spoon awarded to the winner, with no second prize (unless six or more boats) when the winner would buy a drink for the crew of the second boat, and the starter. This action with the formulation of the Club Rules, which now incorporate the rules of the R.Y A. to which the Club was elected in 1948 and became affiliated in 1975; were and are intended to continue to make sailing on the Mere and elsewhere, both safe and exciting.

At this time racing was held every other Sunday afternoon, and in addition the first inter-club competition was held in 1952 against Barnt Green and Sheffield Corinthian Sailing Clubs. These matches were to expand considerably over the next few years with Cadets competing at Burnham Week, Wildcats on Windermere and Fireflysat Opens at Barnt Green. In turn teams visiting the Mere were allowed to change in two of the bedrooms in the Cottage. How the Warden and his family coped with this situation is not on record.

First Race Officer's Box

Training is an ongoing operation, and continues both at the Mere and at other venues, and covers sail training, rescue practice and general race management. In the case of children below the Junior Age Level, this will involve the parents also.

The consequences of Sail Training and Race Programmes at the Club, was to expand competition with other Sailing Clubs and in Open Competition. In 1975 the Club held three Opens which attracted 45 Cadets, 35 Enterprises and 16 Lasers. The Firefly Class was however down to three boats on Trophy Day in 1976.

Testimony to the time and effort put into the Club, by successive members, from the first Sailing Master, through all the Commodores, Committees and loyal members who have helped to organise, or taken part in competitions, is the number of Trophies competed for each season, and the lists of the names of their winners, which are displayed in the Clubhouse.

Entering and winning races not only gives pride of achievement to the individual, but can also bring credit and good publicity to the whole Club. Particularly when National and International participation or honours have been gained by members of Olton Mere Sailing Club.

As far as back as 1974, Liz Clayton was chosen to represent the English Universities against the Welsh, sailing Larks. In 1986 Nicola Pondsford was selected for the British Womens Team in Vancouver, and for the European Laser Championships in Switzerland.

Sailing International Moths requires extra skill and determination, and therefore it is all the more remarkable that Club members have come home with no less than sixteen National, European and World Titles in the space of seventeen years. (1979-1996).

Simon Payne became European Champion in 1994, to be followed in 1998 by Nick Spence who coveted the title in Germany. Roger Angell who had won this same title on no less than four occasions, and in addition was British Champion eight times, and won the World Title twice. What examples for the Junior Sailors to follow.

Add to these achievements, the placing's and appearances of members at Club, Local and National Opens and at Championships, and the picture emerges of the prosperity of Sail Racing within the Club, and also illustrates what can be achieved with proper training and plenty of practice. Not only by the Senior Sailors but by the Juniors also; not forgetting those children below Junior Membership age who sail in the Gold and Silver Fleets, aged six to fourteen years (repeat six to fourteen) boys and girls, and the six year olds are not always last over the line.

The six popular boats now being sailed on the Mere, namely the Enterprise, Laser, Moth, National 12, Optimist and Solo, reflects the changing circumstances of the Club and it's members, particularly over the past fifty years. The design of boats that can be built at home, and the use of modern lightweight materials has allowed enthusiasts not only to build their own boats, but to launch them on to the water more easily; and in many cases allowed transportation by car, an option not originally enjoyed.

These developments have influenced the large increase in competition against other Clubs, both locally and nationally, which augers well for the future of the Olton Mere Sailing Club.

Boats

Boats of many types over the years, been sailed on the Mere to combat the ever changing conditions. Initially sport was non-competitive, the choice of boat was limited and they were expensive. Very little change took place until after the Second World War, except that G.H. Heaton was allowed to moor his Motor Launch in the middle of the Mere, and the story goes, 'that Howard would after Sunday Lunch, row out to this boat in his dinghy, for his afternoon siesta'.

At the time of the formation of the Sailing Section in 1946 the popular boat was the Wildcat, and two Club boats were purchased in 1947, to be adopted as the Club one class design in 1949.

By 1953 the two-man Firefly and the single-handed Enterprise began to arrive on the scene, and by 1962 the Enterprise had replaced the Wildcat, and indeed there were thirty six in the Fleet by 1966. Over this later period the Juniors had been sailing Cadets, with much skill and determination, and were achieving success both on the Mere and at local and national venues. By 1959 the age limit for Juniors was lowered from 16 to 14 years, and by 1960 the Fleet of Cadets numbered ten. Remarkably this boat was to remain popular for a further thirty years until replaced by the Optimist in 1991.

The Optimist which appeared in 1988, has now become the flagship of the Junior Sailing Fleet, and is helping the juniors to continue to develop into national and international competitors.

As racing became even more popular the Solo was tried out in 1963. this boat had particular appeal as it's wooden construction enabled it to be built at home. However, like many other craft it was not long before the fibre-glass version came on to the scene.

In 1967 the Two-man 505 was adopted, but at sixteen feet seven inches in length, and a beam of six feet, this boat proved to be too large for use on the Mere, and was abandoned in 1969.

With the increasing number of single-handed beats on the water, it was only a matter of time before the Canadian designed Laser made it's appearance, which was in 1973. A boat suitable for car-top transportation, this design has proved to be one of the most popular boats ever, particularly due to it's powerful but simple rig.

The National 12 appeared in 1992 as an alternative to the two-handed Lark. Whilst originally designed as long ago as 1936, the use of modern materials, and the wide variations in hull planking arrangements now available, have made this boat as popular as ever. Whilst these changes were taking place the International Moth was gradually increasing in numbers, the first boat appeared in 1979, and in consequence there followed a purple patch of racing success by Club Members, over the following seventeen years, Nationally and Internationally. Certainly this is a boat of the future.

Sailing into the Year 2000

With boats having now sailed the Mere for one hundred years, under the banner of the Olton Mere Club, one would expect not only to see change, but also improvement, possibly coupled with expansion, of the quality of sailing over this period. With membership restricted t the choice of the Lessees for most of the first half century, numbers only increased from eighteen to fifty. In consequence 'quiet controlled seclusion' would not be an inappropriate description, if not of the Club, then certainly of the sailing activity. Like many other aspects of life, World War II was to change members and in turn the Club's ambitions.

Always remembering that the Club had from the beginning, also supported fishing, shooting, bathing and access membership. Sailing enthusiasts requested and were given permission to form their own Sailing (sub) Section in 1946.

This action was to lead to the steady expansion of the Sailing Club. The provision on pontoons, slipways, boat parking space, always necessary but not always adequate, have been built by members over the years, the same with the O.D. Hut. Once the Committee got into it's stride, and having appointed an Honorary Sailing Master, it was not long before Club Rules were formalised to meet Local, National and where appropriate International standards. Officers were elected to oversee Sailing, Safety, Records etc. and as each new Fleet was created so was a Fleet Captain elected, who would then join the Committee. Today there are five Fleet Captains who help plan the Club Programme for the season, oversee races and not only report on results, but make the case for future training, boat repairs and any other expenditure affecting their particular Class. Younger members have always been encouraged on the Committee, and in 1995 the first Lady was welcomed to the Committee to represent yet another growing section of the Club.

The policy of the Sailing Club led by the Commodore and the Committee is to continue to provide an enjoyable and safe environment in which it's members can sail. Whether they are individual sailors, or are interested in racing, the opportunities for basic training and practice are available to all. Certification of all boats is mandatory, which not only gives reassurance to parents of junior sailors, but to all other sailors using the Mere, that safety is a first priority at the Club. Personal competence to sail any class of boat has to be established; once achieved the opportunity to either, race within a Class or train for a higher class of boat is always available.

With membership now well over two hundred, the O.M.S.C. Sailing Programme for the year 2000 will be as full as ever, and with five Fleets competing on the Mere, not forgetting the Moths, the competition will be as keen as ever, and no doubt it will be a year when yet another chapter is added to the long history of Olton Mere Sailing Club.

Wartime

The Lessees or almost anyone else in the country, could not have forecast in 1899 that within fifteen years the nation would be at war. To be repeated again within forty years.

World War I, the so called 'Great War', was to see millions of men killed or injured, fighting on the continent of Europe or at sea. Home support came with everyone trying to do their bit on the land or in the Munitions Factories. Apart from limited bombing raids by airships on the south east of England, and shelling of the east coast by warships; the Home Front effort was concentrated on supporting the troops on the Front Line, rather than self defence.

World War II however, became a global war on land, sea and in the air. Again millions were killed and injured, and many families suffered losses. This time the civilian population were directly involved, due to the threat of invasion, or bombing by enemy aircraft. Strict blackout procedures were imposed on every household, street lighting was severely reduced and shielded, and all car headlights masked to avoid assisting the enemy. These procedures were enforced by both the Police and the Air Raid Wardens.

The general protection of people and property was the responsibility of the Auxiliary Police Force, the Auxiliary Fire Service and the Fire Watchers. The duty of all these organisations was ot only to enforce the 'Blackout' but to ensure that everyone got to the shelters in the event of an air raid, and finally deal with fire bombs and casualties from any large incidents.

Whilst most local bombing occurred in the Birmingham Area, bombs were dropped on Solihull High Street, on Elmdon Heath, where there were fatalities, and two bombs on the railway embankment of the Mere; presumably aimed at the railway line.

Every household was entitled to a Government Issue Air Raid Shelter; the flat-topper Morrison Shelter for use inside buildings, or the Anderson, which was a corrugated curved-topped structure for embedding in the garden.

These shelters ultimately saved many lives, and some families even provided their own luxury versions. For instance a shelter sunk into the back garden of a house in St. Bernards Road on the edge of the Mere was an example. It was thirty feet long by ten feet wide; of concrete construction, with one foot thick beams for the roof, and the whole buried beneath the soil. The floor was carpeted and the walls draped. Self generated lighting and air-conditioning made this shelter comfortable. Remembering that during some periods of the war a family could spend up to twelve hours every night in these structures.

General defence of the country was down to the War Office and the Ministry of Defence who organised the Home Guard. Fomerly known since 1937 as the Local Defence Volunteers, this was a volunteer force who were uniformed and trained initially by the Army. They were fully armed and in the event of an enemy invasion they would be the fist line of defence. Included in their plans locally was to organise a floating boom across the width of the Mere, to prevent enemy aircraft from landing.

A further defence against enemy aircraft was the Balloon Barrage, a protection against low flying raids. These hydrogen-filled balloons were tethered to winch trucks by four hundred metres of steel cable. They were strategically sited to protect important sites and lines of communication. Over one hundred and thirty baloons were sited in the West Midlands. Two local sites were at Braemar Road and St. Bernards (rear of No.44 on the edge of the Mere).

The control of all local sites was from R.A.F. Wythall where over one hundred personnel were engaged in servicing and supplying the operational sites. The Operational Centre was located at Forhill House, where supplies and personnel administration was controlled. It is interesting to note that two of the officers serving some time at this site were, Squadron Leader Kenneth Horne, and Flight Lieutenant Richard Murdoch, of B.B.C. Radio's 'Round the Horne' fame.

During the period 1939-45 the Mere Club, as with many other organisations, helped to raise money for the Red Cross and other War Related Charities. Fishing Contests were held, and full Club support was given on a number of occasions, when Fetes or Garden Parties were held in the gardens of 'Mereside' the home of the Club Chairman C.J. Hurst. A range of boating trips were laid on by members of the Mere Club.

The Grebe Motif

The Club motif in the shape of a pennant, was designed by Life Member John Riley, at the request of the Sailing Committee in 1960, and has since been adopted by the Mere Club. The bird depicted, the Great Crested Grebe, reflects John's keen interest in the birds seen at the Mere during his long and active membership of the Club. This bird possibly the most exotic of twenty six less common birds seen on the Mere; probably not all in one season; the others being the Common Tern, Sandpiper, Black Headed Gull, Cormorant, Mallard, Teal, Widgeon, Pochard, Tufted Duck, Canada Goose, Swan, Heron, Coot, Moorhen, Water Rail, Reedwarbler, Chiff Chaff, Lesser Spotted Woodpecker, Magpie, Pigeon, Tay, Tawny Owl, Jackdaw and Kestrel.

This variety of birds is surely testimony to the condition oand environment maintained at the Mere, both by the Club Lessees and the Committees over the years, and is proof that watersports and the natural habitat can co-exist if managed in an understanding way.

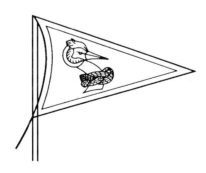

Social Activities

Social activity played a very large part in Victorian life at the turn of the century, especially among those who could afford to entertain. A common used term was 'at home'. Almost everyone had a certain time when they would be at home to callers. Sandwiches and cakes would be set out along with the best tea service, and you dressed to suit the occasion. Should you call at the wrong time you left your 'calling card' or a note on the hall table. This activity was confined mainly to the ladies and usually on weekdays, whereas the businessmen had their dining clubs.

Week ends were usually taken up with the family walking or cycling, and weather permitting the occasional picnic. With the growth of local Charity Groups, and the emergence of many Sports Clubs the pattern began to change.

Woodland walkway, showing water relief channel

The Mere Club not having a Clubhouse in the early years had to rely on good weather to meet socially outside their own homes. The earliest recollections are of wives and children of sailing members, gathering at Florence Bay, when their menfolk would come ashore for an enjoyable picnic lunch or tea.

Local Garden Parties and Fêtes became popular, particularly when used to raise money for charity. Many of these were supported by the Mere Club, and those best remembered were the Garden Parties held in the grounds of 'Mereside' (66 St. Bernards Road, now demolished) which came down to the edge of the Mere. This was the home of a former Chairman of the Club C.J. Hurst, who organised many events in aid of wounded soldiers on local hospitals, the Red Cross and many other local charities.

Numerous sideshows and events were arranged, including boat and canoe trips on the Mere.

Until 1958 any Club social events had to be held outdoors or off-site, as the only meeting point for members was the lounge of the Cottage, and then only for 'taking tea'.

Social Committee

It was on July 27th 1958 that the Clubhouse was duly opened, this being a small alteration to the Cottage. With this facility now available, and the increasing number of families joining the Club, the General Committee decided to create a Social Committee to organise a variety a variety of events to encourage members socially. Members of this Committee have been nominated and elected at the A.G.M. ever since. Made up of a mixture of men and women, but increasingly women who are usually wives or girlfriends of active members. They have tried, and are still trying to arrange more varied and enjoyable events to suit all tastes.

A further step was taken in 1959 when a Bar Committee was formed and Keg Bitter was offered for sale for the first time. The Warden was permitted to sell cigarettes in 1961, and a telephone coin box was installed in 1962.

These facilities, plus more to come were put in place to encourage active and non-active members to meet before and after Club events albeit space was limited. A further extension was completed in 1964, when the now familiar 'bay window' was added, together with additional toilet facilities and a shower room.

Rules for private parties using the Clubhouse were drawn up in 1965, as was the rota for manning the bar on Sundays, due to increased club activities. Bench seats in the bay window increased the capacity in 1966, but the reason for selling the piano in 1968 is not known.

Other than Club Annual Dinner Events held at local pubs or hotels, one of the earliest social events to be organised away from the Club was a 'Trip up the Cut' in 1970. This was to be the forerunner of many events to follow, however, one event to effect the whole Club in general, and the Social Committee in particular, was the major extension to the Clubhouse in 1975. Not only were the toilet, changing and shower facilities improved, but the accommodation for socialising was also enlarged. Add to this event the addition of a Pool Table in 1978, the installation of central heating in 1980, and the 'Committee' could now really get to work.

This they did, and what followed was a series of events, mainly non energetic, for young and old, and as always, hopefully to suit all tasts. In 1978 and 1980 there were pig roasts, followed in 1979 by a Chinese Evening, and Tramps and Ploughman's Suppers.

A Harvesters Ball was organised in 1980, to be followed over the years by food and drink events, to suit your taste or nationality. There have been Greek, Chinese, Indian, Scottish and Carribean Evenings. For the connoisseur, a Wine and Cheese Party, Food for Thought and Paté and Plonk. A Childrens' Christmas Party and a Pensioners' Afternoon followed by a Valentines Party, were aimed at the young and old alike. The New Members' Nights have proved very popular, and the Ladies' Makeover Night was a lot of fun.

All these types of event are still continuing up to the present time, and if you have not 'heard about them' - complain, and if your kind of event is not in sight, see the secretary.

Not all socialising at the Club is organised or necessarily in large numbers, many visitors come to watch the sailing, walk the grounds or sit and enjoy a drink at the bar, usually with friends or relations.

Over the years and particularly since 1958, when Dr. Cartwright presented the first Vistors' Book, the hometown locations of visitors have been recorded. The whole of the British Isles is represented including the Channel Isles. What is surprising is that names from twenty four countries and five continents are entered in the book.

Hopefully all will have been impressed with the beauty of the Mere and the surrounding tree lined banks.

Many local residents have been Club Members, or visitors, and particularly those whose properties overlook the Mere. One such property was newlyn, 32 St. Bernards Road. Here in 1911 lived Georgie and Arthur Gaskin, who were famous Book Illustrators, and designers of silver and jewellery.

A frequent visitor to this household was John Drinkwater, Poet and Playwright and Manager of the forerunner of the Birmingham Rep. The result of his many visits to both the Gaskins home, and the Mere was that he was so impressed with it's beauty, he composed a poem entitled '*Olton Pools*' and dedicated it to the Gaskins. But not only was the poem entitled, but the whole volume was entitled '*Olton Pools*' (see frontispiece). After this work, and others were published John Drinkwater became nationally and internationally famous. How many people, having read this poem, have asked the question, do Olton Pools exist, and if so where are they?

Grebe Investment Club / The Meremaids

In 1964 a small group of members decided to form the first of the Grebe Investment Clubs. The Investment Club idea was gaining ground throughout the country, although at that time it was nothing like as widespread as it subsequently became. Each 'Club' had a life of five years, after which period a new Club was formed, some members dropping out, while others joined, the main requirement apart from, of course, the maintenance of the specified monthly subscription, being membership of Olton Mere Club. At this time, Grebe Investment Club Seven is in it's ultimate year, and over the period of thirty plus years, each Club has shown a profit for it's members, sometimes meagre, but generally sufficiently encouraging to warrant continued succession. The main benefits have been the bringing together of members in a specialised way, the stimulation of thoughtful conversation, and, on occasion, enjoying visits by speakers on kindred subjects, with the additional feature of quarterly dinners, to one of which, each year, members ladies have been invited.

Until 1980 interest had been monopolised by males of Olton Mere Club, but in that year, some of the ladies decided to follow their example, and a group, calling itself ' The Ladymere Investment

Club', was formed. The name was subsequently changed to 'The Meremaids', and, over the years, the intelligence and judgement of members have proved to be formidable and generally consistantly profitable investments have resulted from their discussions. As with their male counterparts, their activities have been beneficial socially, both for the parent Club, and individually for the members concerned. A wide range of speakers has been one of the features of their meetings, and, among other activities, a day as Ascot was arranged in 1996.

Epilogue

As Olton Mere Club embarks into its Second Century, maybe we should reflect for a few moments and consider the events and people who have laid down the markers on a story of success.

The first that come to mind are of course the original Lessees, who as a group of five created the Club, and set it on its way. Not only did they formulate the rules of membership, but in some instances provided facilities such as bench-seats, pontoons and fish stocks at their own expense. They not only made early provision for the enjoyment of the members, but some stayed with the Club long enough to negotiate a second and even a third extension of the Lease, taking the Club into the 1930s.

Following this first initative, subsequent Lessees and General Committee Members have unselfishly given their time, (and often their money) in promoting the cause of the Club and its members. Whilst the formative years were of relative low activity, skating, shooting and bathing were included in pastimes offered, and these had to be controlled, if only to satisfy the neighbours whose properties were beginning to surround the Mere.

With the explosion of membership of all types of sporting club after the Second World War, the creation of both the Fishing and Sailing Sections within the Mere Club, was in hindsight one of the three major events in the history of the Club. Not only did the membership increase, but activities both inside and outside the Clud widened. fishing was expanded with the provision of the many permanent platforms around the Mere banks, encouraging the individual angler as well as the members who enjoy the regular Club Contests, and those against local Clubs. Again the youngsters were not forgotten, as when the local Scout Troop take their Fishing Badge.

Sailing having survived as an individual pastime since the turn of the century, like fishing, came 'alive' in 1946. With its own sub-committee, the Sailing Section set out its rules for sailing and safety. Good organisation and extensive training resulted in what has become a full Annual Race Programme, including competition outside the Club, locally, nationally and internationally. The many awards gained over the years are testimony to the organisation, training and skills of those Officers and Members who have worked hard to create the Sailing Club it is today.

Following the original formation of the Club, and the creation of the Fishing and Sailing Sections, the third major milestone of the century was the final enlargement of the Clubhouse in 1975. This event immediately widened the scope of the Club to entertain both members and visitors alike, at sporting and social events and has helped to create the wide reputation the Club enjoys today.

Social activities have expanded over the years in line with the increase in membership. Whilst attendance at Annual General Meetings of the Mere Club, or thetwo sub-sections have not exactly been 'standing roon only' over the years; the large attendance at the Annual Fishing Club Presentation Evening and the Sailing Club Laying-Up Supper, bear testimony to the strong support enjoyed by these two sections. However, the many events organised by the Social Committee are not confined to sailing or fishing. If you eat, drink, enjoy music and good company, are young, old or somewhere in the middle, the committee have continued to vary their programme to meet all ages and tastes.

Some members have over the years, and continue to this day to enjoy a quiet drink in the Clubhouse, or chat with friends, with no intention of physical activity of any kind, except maybe a walk round the Mere for the exercise or to admire the view and the wildlife.

So on reflection it is the successors to the original Lessees, the Committees, Presidents, Chairmen, Secretaries, Treasurers and Officers, who have served the Club so well, that we have to thank, together with all those members both past and present (not forgetting the existing Life Members) who have, not only enjoyed their membership, but have gome on to bring honour to the Club, or have worked to enable others to do so.

And the next One Hundred Years......Tell your grandchildren to watch this space.

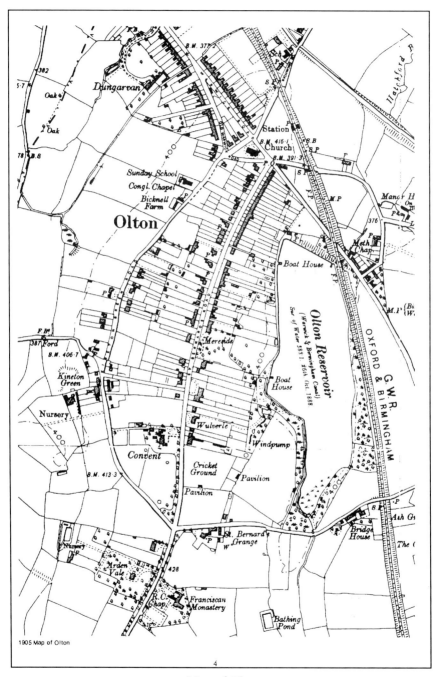

1905 Map of Olton

4

Map of Olton

52

Sailing on Olton Mere

Telegram from King Edward VIII (Duke of Windsor) - occasion Diamond Wedding Anniversary of Mark & Annie Mintram

References

Tithe Schedule	1840
Bickenhill Tithe Map	1839
Solihull Tithe Map	1837
The Warwick Canals	Alan Faulkner
Discovering Bickenhill	Victor Skipp
Olton Heritage	Jordan/Powrie/
	Andrews
The Birmingham Canal Navigation	S. Broadbridge
The History of Midland Waterways	Hodgkinson
Warwick Record Office	
British Inland Waterways - Glos.	R. Jamieson
Barrage Balloon Re-Union Club	
Teletext - Service Pals	
Solihull Reference Library	S. Bates
Birmingham Reference Library	
Acocks Green Reference Library	
Olton Reference Library	
Sheldon Reference Library	
Wythall Council Office	

Further Acknowledgements

Map of Olton	By kind permission of H.M. Stationery Office. Crown Copyright.
Photographs	Night Sailing by kind permission of Rod Embley, F.R.P.S.
	Mark and Anne Mintram by kind permission of Mrs. Joan Bradley.
	Others by kind permission of Solihull Education, Libraries and Arts Dept.
Poem - Olton Pools	By kind permission of Samuel French Ltd. on behalf of the estate of John Drinkwater.